A BIBLIOGRAPHY OF MODERN
IRISH DRAMA 1899–1970

A BIBLIOGRAPHY OF MODERN IRISH DRAMA
1899–1970

E. H. MIKHAIL

With a foreword by
WILLIAM A. ARMSTRONG

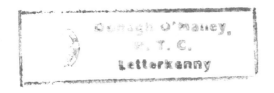
MACMILLAN

First published 1972 by
THE MACMILLAN PRESS LTD
London and Basingstoke
Associated companies in New York Toronto
Dublin Melbourne Johannesburg and Madras

SBN 333 14024 9

Printed in Great Britain by
R. & R. CLARK LTD
Edinburgh

Contents

Foreword

In 1999 – twenty-seven years hence – the Irish National Theatre will celebrate its first centenary. Its history, no less thanthe drama to which it is dedicated, has abounded in ironies, vicissitudes and affirmations of faith in the vision without which a people perishes. One of the distinctive merits of a good literary bibliography is that it enables us to chart in detail these adventures of the human imagination with their inevitable ebbs and flows, vagaries and virtues, eccentricities and grandeurs. In recent years no bibliographer has rendered better service of this kind to the Irish Dramatic Movement than Professor Edward Mikhail. His valuable survey, 'Sixty Years of Synge Criticism, 1907-1967' in *Bulletin of Bibliography* (1971) has been followed by his authoritative *Sean O'Casey: A Bibliography of Criticism* (1972) and by the present work, which is the first comprehensive bibliography of general studies of Irish Drama written between 1899 and 1970.

The reader who follows the accurate and well-organised leads given by Professor Mikhail's bibliography will be amply rewarded. Among other things, it shows that Irish Drama has had its Jeremiahs in almost every decade of its existence. In 1912, G. Hamilton Gunning was lamenting 'The Decline of Abbey Theatre Drama': in 1925, A. E. Malone bewailed 'The Decline of the Irish Drama': in 1935, Hugh Smith posed his pessimistic question, 'Twilight of the Abbey?', and in 1951 Dr Irving D. Suss completed a dissertation on 'The Decline and Fall of Irish Drama'. But the corpse at these wakes, like the famous Finnegan's, has refused to lie down; O'Casey's resurgent genius has belied Malone's epitaph just as Brendan Behan's has Dr Suss's. Moreover, the word 'decline' in their epitaphs postulates the existence of positive and vital achievements at certain stages of the Irish Dramatic Movement. Other items in Professor Mikhail's bibliography bear lively witness to the strong attraction which these achievements have had for some of the ablest dramatic critics, the most original personalities, the finest scholars, and the most cosmopolitan sensibilities during the past seventy years, for it notes the characteristic contributions to the understanding of Irish Drama made by such rich and diverse minds as those of Max Beerbohm, A. B. Walkley, C. E. Montague, W. J. Lawrence, John Masefield, Theodore Roosevelt, and Charles Tennyson in its early days, and those of George Jean Nathan, E. K. Chambers, Carl and Mark van Doren, James T. Farrell, and Eric Bentley in more recent times. As these names indicate, Professor Mikhail's bibliography is a valuable contribution to the history of taste as well as a tribute to the enduring appeal of Irish Drama, and on both counts deserves our gratitude and our regular recourse to its guidance.

WILLIAM A. ARMSTRONG

Westfield College,
University of London

Preface

The theatre is not a native institution of Ireland, and there is no record of dramatic performances prior to the mystery or miracle play of the sixteenth century. The eighteenth century saw a great blaze of dramatic talent in Dublin, but the Dublin playgoer of the day was so imbued with the Anglicising influences that he would not support the native dramatist until his work had obtained the hallmark of London approval. On the other hand, the budding native player was received with every sign of encouragement and approbation before he had won his spurs on the boards of the English stage. It is worth while recalling that the player invariably repaid this kindness by betaking himself to London at the earliest opportunity, only revisiting his native land at long intervals. From these circumstances it was impossible to build up a native drama, and it was not until the establishment of the National Theatre movement in 1899 that any serious steps were taken to build a native drama for Ireland.

Studies of modern Irish drama have recently been on the increase, and a bibliography of criticism is overdue. Checklists and selected bibliographies have appeared separately or incorporated in books and periodicals. These however are either selective, or deal mainly with individual playwrights. The present work, which comprises some 600 entries, is the first attempt towards a comprehensive general bibliography. It was written in an effort to bring up to date and consolidate in one volume all the existing bibliographies containing secondary material, plus the addition of many new items – never before compiled – that resulted from personal research in major libraries during the past few years. It covers a period from

1899, with the foundation of the Irish Literary Theatre, to the end of 1970, although some later studies have been included. Entries have been annotated only when the title does not give any suggestion of the nature of the material involved or when information is necessary to supplement the title.

To Dr Ronald Ayling I owe thanks for his perceptive and discriminating judgments and his many helpful comments. I am also indebted to the staff of the University of Lethbridge Library; the British Museum Library; the Newspaper Library, Colindale; the British Drama League Library, London; Trinity College Library, Dublin; The National Library of Ireland, Dublin; and Queen's University Library, Belfast.

The following bibliographical aids have been checked to set up the groundwork of my Bibliography:

Abstracts of English Studies, 1958– (Boulder, Col.: National Council of Teachers of English).

Annual Bibliography of English Language and Literature, 1920– (London: Modern Humanities Research Association).

Cambridge Bibliography of English Literature, 5 vols. (Cambridge: Cambridge University Press).

Cumulative Book Index, 1928– (New York: H. W. Wilson).

Dissertation Abstracts, 1938– (Ann Arbor, Mich.: University Microfilms).

Dissertations in English and American Literature; Theses Accepted by American, British and German Universities, 1865-1964, by Lawrence F. McNamee (New York and London: R. R. Bowker, 1968).

Doctoral Dissertations Accepted by American Universities, ed. Arnold H. Trotier and Marian Harman (New York: H. W. Wilson, 1933–1955). Continued as *Index to American Doctoral Dissertations*, 1955– .

Dramatic Index, 1909–1949 (Boston: F. W. Faxon).

Essay and General Literature Index, 1900– (New York: H. W. Wilson).

Index to Little Magazines, 1943– (Denver: Alan Swallow).

Index to One-Act Plays, comp. by Hannah Logasa and Winifred Ver Nooy (Boston: F. W. Faxon, 1924); *Supplement, 1924–1931* (Boston: F. W. Faxon, 1932); *Second Supplement, 1932–1940* (Boston; F. W. Faxon, 1941); *Third Supplement, 1941–1948*

(Boston: F. W. Faxon, 1950); *Fourth Supplement, 1948–1957* (Boston: F. W. Faxon, 1958).

Index to Plays 1800–1926, comp. by Ina Ten Eyck Firkins (New York: H. W. Wilson, 1927).

Index to plays, Supplement, comp. by Ina Ten Eyck Firkins (New York: H. W. Wilson, 1935).

Index to Plays in Collections, ed. John H. Ottemiller (Washington: The Scarecrow Press, 1951).

Index to Theses Accepted for Higher Degrees in the Universities of Great Britain and Ireland, 1950– (London: ASLIB).

International Index to Periodicals, 1907– (New York: H. W. Wilson). From vol. 19 (Apr 1965–Mar 1966) called *Social Sciences and Humanities Index*.

Masters Abstracts, 1962– (Ann Arbor, Mich.: University Microfilms).

New York Times Index.

PMLA Bibliography.

Play Index 1949–1952; An Index to 2626 Plays in 1138 Volumes, comp. by Dorothy Herbert West and Dorothy Margaret Peake (New York: H. W. Wilson, 1953).

Readers' Guide to Periodical Literature, 1900– (New York: H. W. Wilson).

Subject Index to Periodicals, 1915–1961 (London: The Library Association). Continued as *British Humanities Index*, 1962–.

Theatre Dissertations, ed. Frederic M. Litto (Kent: Kent State University Press, 1969).

The Times Index.

Year's Work in English Studies, 1919– (London: The English Association).

E. H. MIKHAIL

Lethbridge,
September 1971

1. Bibliographies

ADELMAN, IRVING and RITA DWORKIN, *Modern Drama; A Checklist of Critical Literature on 20th Century Plays* (Metuchen, N.J.: The Scarecrow Press, 1967).

BATESON, F. W. (ed.), 'Anglo-Irish Literature', *The Cambridge Bibliography of English Literature. Volume III: 1800–1900* (Cambridge: Cambridge University Press, 1940) pp. 1045–1067; *Supplement* (Cambridge: Cambridge University Press, 1957) pp. 698–706.

BOYD, ERNEST A., 'Bibliographical Appendix', *The Contemporary Drama of Ireland* (Dublin: Talbot Press; London: T. Fisher Unwin, 1918; Boston: Little, Brown, 1928) pp. 201–11.

'Bibliography', *Ireland's Literary Renaissance* (New York: Alfred A. Knopf, 1922) pp. 401–15.

BROWN, STEPHEN J. (ed.), *A Guide to Books on Ireland* (London: Longmans, Green; Dublin: Hodges, Figgis, 1912).

COLEMAN, ARTHUR and GARY TYLER, *Drama Criticism, Vol. I: A Checklist of Interpretation Since 1940 of English and American Plays* (Denver: Alan Swallow, 1966).

EAGER, ALAN R., *A Guide to Irish Bibliographical Material;
Being a Bibliography of Irish Bibliographies and Some Sources
of Information* (London: The Library Association, 1964).

Encyclopedia of Ireland (Dublin: Allen Figgis, 1968).

FRENCH, FRANCES-JANE, *A Bibliography of the Tower Press
Booklets* (London: Athlone Press, 1968).
The Abbey Theatre Series of Plays; A Bibliography (Dublin:
The Dolmen Press, 1969).

HARMON, MAURICE, *Modern Irish Literature, 1800–1967; A
Reader's Guide* (Dublin: The Dolmen Press, 1967).

HOGAN, ROBERT, 'Bibliography', *After the Irish Renaissance;
A Critical History of the Irish Drama Since 'The Plough and
the Stars'* (Minneapolis: University of Minnesota Press,
1967; London: Macmillan, 1968) pp. 259–74.

LEARY, LEWIS (ed.), *Contemporary Literary Scholarship; A
Critical Review* (New York: Appleton-Century-Crofts,
1958) pp. 331–3.

MACNAMARA, BRINSLEY (ed.), *Abbey Plays 1899–1948.
Including the Productions of the Irish Literary Theatre* (Dublin: At the Sign of the Three Candles [1949]).

MILLER, ANNA IRENE, 'Ireland', *The Independent Theatre in
Europe 1887 to the Present* (New York: R. Long & R. R.
Smith, 1931; Benjamin Blom, 1966) pp. 396–400.

O'DONOGHUE, D. J., *The Poets of Ireland; A Biographical and
Bibliographical Dictionary* (Dublin: Hodges, Figgis, 1912).

O'MAHONY, MATHEW, *Guide to Anglo-Irish Plays* (Dublin:
Progress House, 1960).

BIBLIOGRAPHIES

O'NEILL, JAMES J., *A Bibliographical Account of Irish Theatrical Literature*. Bibliographical Society of Ireland Publications. Vol. I, No. 6 (Dublin: John Falconer, 1920).

PALMER, HELEN H. and ANNE JANE DYSON (comps.), *European Drama Criticism* (Hamden, Conn.: The Shoe String Press, 1968).

SALEM, JAMES M., *A Guide to Critical Reviews, Part III: British and Continental Drama from Ibsen to Pinter* (Metuchen, N.J.: The Scarecrow Press, 1968).

YOUNG, DEREK (ed.), *Stagecast Directory* (Dublin: Stagecast, published annually from 1962).

2. Books

'ABBEY THEATRE', *The New Funk & Wagnalls Encyclopedia*, vol. I (New York: Unicorn Publishers, 1950) pp. 11–12.

'THE ABBEY THEATRE', *The Ireland of Today, Reprinted, with Some Additions, from The London Times* (London: John Murray, 1913; Boston: Small Maynard, 1915), Part III, chap. V, pp. 131–7.

Abbey Theatre 1904–1966 (Dublin: The National Theatre Society, [1966]) [brochure].

ANDREWS, CHARLTON, *The Drama Today* (Philadelphia and London: J. B. Lippincott, 1913) pp. 160–8.

ARMSTRONG, W. A., 'The Irish Point of View: The Plays of Sean O'Casey, Brendan Behan, and Thomas Murphy', *Experimental Drama* (London: G. Bell, 1963).

'The Irish Dramatic Movement', *Classic Irish Drama* (Harmondsworth: Penguin, 1964).

BARNET, SYLVAN, MORTON BERMAN and WILLIAM BURTON (eds.), 'The Irish Theater: An Introduction'. *The Genius of the Irish Theatre.* Mentor Books (New York: The New American Library, 1960).

BEACH, JOSEPH WARREN, 'The Drama in Ireland', *English Literature of the Nineteenth and the Early Twentieth Centuries: 1798 to the First World War* vol. IV of *A History of English Literature*, gen. ed. Hardin Craig (New York: Collier Books; London: Collier-Macmillan, 1966) pp. 221–6.

BECKERMAN, BERNARD, *Dynamics of Drama, Theory and Method of Analysis* (New York: Alfred A. Knopf, 1970).

BEERBOHM, MAX, *Around Theatres* (London: Rupert Hart-Davis, 1953).

'In Dublin', *The Genius of the Irish Theatre*, ed. Barnet *et al.* Mentor Books (New York: The New American Library, 1960).

BELL, SAM HANNA, 'Theatre', *Causeway: The Arts in Ulster*, (ed.) Michael Longley (Belfast: Arts Council of Northern Ireland, 1971) pp. 83–94.

BENTLEY, ERIC, *The Dramatic Event* (New York: Horizon Press, 1954; Boston: Beacon Press, 1956).
What is Theatre? (London: Dobson, 1957).
In Search of Theater (New York: Vintage Books, 1953).
The Modern Theatre: A Study of Dramatists and the Drama (London: Robert Hale, 1948).

BICKLEY, FRANCIS, *J. M. Synge and the Irish Dramatic Movement* (London: Constable; Boston and New York: Houghton Mifflin, 1912).

BLACK, HESTER M., *The Theatre in Ireland: An Introductory Essay* (Dublin: Trinity College, 1957).

BLUNT, JERRY, 'Irish', *Stage Dialects* (San Francsico, Calif.: Chandler Publishing Company, 1967) chap. viii.

BLYTHE, ERNEST, *The Abbey Theatre* (Dublin: The National Theatre Society, [1965]).

BOGARD, TRAVIS and WILLIAM I. OLIVER (eds.), *Modern Drama: Essays in Criticism.* Galaxy Books (New York: Oxford University Press, 1965).

BORSA, MARIO, 'The Irish National Theatre', *The English Stage of Today.* Translated by Selwyn Brinton (London and New York: John Lane, 1908) pp. 286–314.

BOURGEOIS, MAURICE, *J. M. Synge and the Irish Theatre*

(London: Constable, 1912; Bronx, N.Y.: Benjamin Blom, 1965; New York: Haskell House, 1966).

BOYD, ERNEST A., *Appreciations and Depreciations: Irish Literary Studies* (Dublin: Talbot Press, 1917; London: T. Fisher Unwin; New York: John Lane, 1918).

The Contemporary Drama of Ireland (Dublin: Talbot Press; London: T. Fisher Unwin, 1918; Boston: Little, Brown, 1928).

Ireland's Literary Renaissance (Dublin: Talbot Press, 1916, New York: Alfred A. Knopf, 1922; Dublin: Allen Figgis, 1968).

BRADBROOK, M. C., 'Yeats and the Revival', *English Dramatic Form: A History of Its Development* (London: Chatto & Windus, 1965) chap. 7.

BRAWLEY, BENJAMIN, 'Irish National Theatre, '*A Short History of the English Drama* (London: George G. Harrap, [1921]) pp. 230–4.

BROOK, DONALD, 'Irish Creation and Provincial Awakening', *The Romance of the English Theatre* (London: Rockliff, 1952) pp. 166–70.

BROOKS, VAN WYCK, 'Impressions of Ireland', *From the Shadow of the Mountain: My Post-Meridian Years* (New York: E. P. Dutton; Toronto: Clarke, Irwin, 1961), pp. 138–61.

BRYANT, SOPHIE, 'The Gael in Literature', *The Genius of the Gael: A Study in Celtic Psychology and Its Manifestations* (London: T. Fisher Unwin, 1913) chap. vi, pp. 181–218.

BURTON, E. J., *The Student's Guide to British Theatre and Drama* (London: Herbert Jenkins, 1963) pp. 150–56.

BYRNE, DAWSON, *The Story of Ireland's National Theatre: The Abbey Theatre, Dublin* (Dublin: Talbot Press, 1929).

CANFIELD, CURTIS (ed.), *Plays of the Irish Renaissance* (New York: Macmillan, 1929).

(ed.), *Plays of Changing Ireland* (New York: Macmillan, 1936).

CARNEY, JAMES, *Studies in Irish Literature and History* (Dublin: Dublin Institute for Advanced Studies, 1955).

CARTMELL, VAN H. (ed.), *Plot Outlines of 100 Famous Plays*. Dolphin Books (Garden City, N.Y.: Doubleday, 1962).

CHANDLER, FRANK WADLEIGH, *Aspects of Modern Drama* (New York: Macmillan, 1927).

CHESTERTON, G. K., *Irish Impressions* (London: W. Collins, 1919; New York: John Lane, 1920).

CHEW, SAMUEL C. and RICHARD D. ALTICK, 'The Irish Literary Renaissance', *The Nineteenth Century and After, 1789–1939*, Vol. IV of *A Literary History of England* (ed.), Albert C. Baugh (New York: Appleton-Century-Crofts, 1948) pp. 1507–15.

CHIARI, J., *Landmarks of Contemporary Drama* (London: Herbert Jenkins, 1965).

CHISHOLM, CECIL, *Repertory: An Outline of the Modern Theatre Movement* (London: Peter Davis, 1934).

CLARK, BARRETT H., 'The Irish Drama', *The British and American Drama of Today* (New York: Holt, 1915; Cincinnati: Steward & Kidd, 1921; New York: Scribner's, 1930; New York: AMS Press, 1971).
'The Irish Drama', *A Study of Modern Drama* (New York and London: A. Appleton-Century, 1934).

CLARK, WILLIAM S., 'The Rise of the Irish Theater and Drama', *Chief Patterns of World Drama: Aeschylus to Anderson* (Boston: Houghton Mifflin, 1946) pp. 887–90.

COHEN, HELEN LOUISE, 'The Irish National Theater', *One-Act Plays by Modern Authors* (New York: Harcourt, Brace, 1921).

COLE, TOBY (ed.), *Playwrights on Playwriting: The Meaning and Making of Modern Drama from Ibsen to Ionesco*. Introduction by John Gassner. A Dramabook (New York: Hill & Wang, 1961).

COLLINS, A. S. 'The Drama, 1900 to 1950', *English Literature of the 20th Century* (London: University Tutorial Press, 1965) pp. 289–302.

COLUM, MARY, *Life and the Dream* (London: Macmillan, 1947).

COLUM, PADRAIC, *My Irish Year* (London: Mills & Boon, 1912).

The Road Round Ireland (New York: Macmillan, 1926).

COQUELIN, C., *The Art of the Actor* (London: Allen & Unwin, 1932).

CORKERY, DANIEL, *Synge and Anglo-Irish Literature: A Study* (Dublin and Cork: Cork University Press; London: Longmans, Green, 1931; Cork: Mercier Press, 1966).

CORRIGAN, ROBERT W. (ed.), 'The Irish Dramatic Flair', *Masterpieces of the Modern Irish Theatre* (New York: Collier, 1967).

COURTNEY, SISTER MARIE-THERESE, *Edward Martyn and the Irish Theatre* (New York: Vantage Press, 1956).

COWELL, RAYMOND, 'The Irish Contribution', *Twelve Modern Dramatists* (Oxford: Pergamon Press, 1967), pp. 49–75.

COXHEAD, ELIZABETH. *Lady Gregory: A Literary Portrait* (London: Macmillan, 1961).

J. M. Synge and Lady Gregory. Writers and Their Work: No. 149 (London: Longmans, Green, for The British Council and The National Book League, 1962).

Daughters of Erin: Five Women of the Irish Renascence (London: Secker & Warburg, 1965).

CUNLIFFE, J. W., *Modern English Playwrights: A Short History of the English Drama from 1825* (London and New York: Harper, 1927; Port Washington, N.Y.: Kennikat Press, 1969) pp. 100–24.

'The Irish Renaissance', *English Literature in the Twentieth Century* (New York: Macmillan, 1933).

'The Irish Movement', *English Literature During the Last Half-Century* (New York: Macmillan, 1925; Freeport, N.Y.: Books for Libraries Press, 1971) pp. 249–70.

CURRAN, C. P., *Under the Receding Wave* (London: Gill & Macmillan, 1970).

DAY, MARTIN S., 'The Celtic Renaissance and Irish Literature to the Present', *History of English Literature, 1837 to the Present* (Garden City, N.Y.: Doubleday, 1964).

DICKINSON, THOMAS H., 'Playwrights of the Irish Theatre', *An Outline of Contemporary Drama* (Boston: Houghton Mifflin, 1927; New York: Biblo & Tannen, 1969) pp. 226–8.

DOBRÉE, BONAMY, 'Sean O'Casey and the Irish Drama', *Sean O'Casey*, ed. Ronald Ayling (London: Macmillan, 1969).

DONOGHUE, DENIS, *The Third Voice: Modern British and American Verse Drama* (London: Oxford University Press; Princeton, N.J.: Princeton University Press, 1959).

DRIVER, TOM F., *Romantic Quest and Modern Query; A History of the Modern Theatre* (New York: Dell, 1970).

DRURY, FRANCIS K. W., *Drury's Guide to Best Plays*, second edition, ed. James M. Salem (Metuchen, N.J.: The Scarecrow Press, 1969).

DUGGAN, G. C., *The Stage Irishman; A History of the Irish Play and Stage Characters from the Earliest Times* (Dublin and Cork: Talbot Press; London: Longmans, 1937).

DUKES, ASHLEY, *The Youngest Drama; Studies of Fifty Dramatists* (Chicago: Charles H. Sergel, 1924; Folcroft, Pa.: The Folcroft Press, 1969).

EATON, WALTER PRITCHARD, ' "Local" Drama and the

Irish Revival – Synge and O'Casey', *The Drama in English* (New York: Scribner's, 1930).

EDWARDS, HILTON, *The Mantle of Harlequin*. With a Preface and Two Designs by Micheál Mac Liammóir (Dublin: Progress House, 1958).

EGLINTON, JOHN, 'What Should Be the Subjects of National Drama?' *Literary Ideals in Ireland* (London: Fisher Unwin, 1899).
Irish Literary Portraits (London: Macmillan, 1935).

ELLIS-FERMOR, UNA, *The Irish Dramatic Movement* (London: Methuen, 1939; University Paperbacks, 1967).
The Frontiers of Drama (London: Methuen, 1945; University Paperbacks, 1964).

ELTON, OLIVER, 'Living Irish Literature', *Modern Studies* (London: Edward Arnold, 1907).

Encyclopedia of Ireland (Dublin: Allen Figgis, 1968).

ERVINE, ST. JOHN, *Some Impressions of My Elders* (London: George Allen & Unwin, 1923).
The Theatre in My Time (London: Rich & Cowan, 1933).

EVANS, SIR IFOR, *A Short History of English Drama* (Harmondsworth, Penguin Books, 1948); second edition, rev. and enl. (Boston: Houghton Mifflin, 1965).

FALLON, GABRIEL (ed.), *Abbey Theatre 1904–1966* (Dublin: National Theatre Society, 1966).
The Abbey and the Actor (Dublin: National Theatre Society, 1969).

FAY, FRANK J., *Towards a National Theatre: Dramatic Criticism*, ed. with an Introduction by Robert Hogan (Dublin: Dolmen Press, 1970).

FAY, GERARD, *The Abbey Theatre, Cradle of Genius* (Dublin: Clonmore & Reynolds; London: Hollis & Carter, 1958).

'Abbey Theatre', *Encyclopaedia Britannica*, vol. 1 (London: Encyclopaedia Britannica, 1970), p. 11.

'Abbey Theatre', *The Encyclopedia Americana*, International Edition, vol. 1 (New York: Americana Corporation, 1969) p. 13.

FAY, WILLIAM GEORGE, *Mainly Players* (London: Rich & Cowan, 1932).

and CATHERINE CARSWELL, *The Fays of the Abbey Theatre* (London: Rich & Cowan; New York: Harcourt, Brace, 1935).

FIGGIS, DARRELL, *Studies and Appreciations* (London: J. M. Dent; New York: Dutton, 1912).

FINDLATER, RICHARD, *The Unholy Trade* (London: Victor Gollancz, 1952).

FLANAGAN, HALLIE, 'Erin', *Shifting Scenes of the Modern European Theatre* (New York: Coward-McCann, 1928; London: Harrap, 1929).

FLANNERY, JAMES, *Miss Annie F. Horniman and the Abbey Theatre* (Dublin: Dolmen Press, 1970).

FRASER, G. S., 'The Irish Dramatic Revival', *The Modern Writer and His World* (Harmondsworth: Penguin, 1964).

FREEDLEY, GEORGE, 'The Irish Revival', *The World Book Encyclopedia*, vol. 5 (Chicago: Field Enterprises Educational Corporation, 1966) p. 272.

FREYER, GRATTAN, 'The Irish Contribution', *The Modern Age*. The Pelican Guide to English Literature, 7, ed. by Boris Ford (Harmondsworth: Penguin, 1961).

GASCOIGNE, BAMBER, *Twentieth Century Drama* (London: Hutchinson University Library, 1962).

GASSNER, JOHN, 'Abbey Theatre', *The World Book Encyclopedia* (Chicago: Field Enterprises Educational Corporation, 1966) p. 6.

Masters of the Drama (New York: Random House, 1940) chap. xxvii.

The Theatre in Our Times (New York: Crown Publishers, 1954).

and EDWARD QUINN (eds.), *The Reader's Encyclopedia of World Drama* (London: Methuen, 1970).

GOGARTY, OLIVER ST. JOHN, *As I was Going Down Sackville Street* (London: Reynal; New York: Ryerson Press, 1937; London: Sphere Books, 1968).

GOLDMAN, EMMA, 'The Irish Drama', *The Social Significance of the Modern Drama* (Boston: Richard G. Badger; Toronto: Copp Clark, 1914).

GORELIK, MORDECAI, *New Theatres for Old* (London: Dobson, 1947).

GRAVES, A. P., 'Anglo-Irish Literature', *The Cambridge History of English Literature*, vol. XIV, ed. A. W. Ward and A. R. Waller (Cambridge: Cambridge University Press, 1964) pp. 329–30.

GREENE, DAVID H., 'Irish Literary Revival', *The Encyclopedia Americana*, International Edition, vol. 15 (New York: Americana Corporation, 1969) pp. 420–23.

(ed.), *An Anthology of Irish Literature* (New York: Modern Library, 1954: New York: University Press, 1971).

GREGORY, LADY ISABELLA AUGUSTA, *Our Irish Theatre* (New York and London: G. P. Putnam, 1914; New York: Capricorn Books, 1965).

Poets and Dreamers (Dublin: Hodges, Figgis, 1903).

(ed.), *Ideals in Ireland* (London: At the Unicorn, 1907).

Journals 1916–1930, ed. Lennox Robinson (London: Putnam, 1946).

GUTHRIE, TYRONE, 'Ireland', *A Life in the Theatre* (New York and London: McGraw-Hill, 1959).

GWYNN, DENIS, 'The Irish Literary Theatre', *Edward Martyn and the Irish Revival* (London: Jonathan Cape, 1930).

GWYNN, STEPHEN, 'The Gaelic League and the Irish Theatre' *Today and Tomorrow in Ireland; Essays on Irish Subjects* (Dublin: Hodges, Figgis; London: Macmillan, 1903) pp. 87–96 [Adapted from an article in *The Westminster Gazette*, with extracts from one in *The Fortnightly Review*].

Irish Books and Irish People (Dublin: Talbot Press; London: T. Fisher Unwin, n.d. [1920]).

Irish Literature and Drama in the English Language: A Short History (London: Thomas Nelson, 1936; Folcroft, Pa.: The Folcroft Press, 1969).

'The Irish Theatre', *Irish Literature*, ed. by Justin MacCarthy (Chicago: John D. Morris – The de Bower Elliot Co., 1904).

HAMILTON, CLAYTON, 'The Irish National Theatre', *Studies in Stagecraft* (London: Grant Richards; New York: Henry Holt, 1914) pp. 123–44.

HARTNOLL, PHYLLIS (ed.), *The Oxford Companion to the Theatre* (London: Oxford University Press, 1967).

HENDERSON, W. A., *1909: The Irish National Theatre Movement. A Year's Work at the Abbey Theatre. Events: Death of J. M. Synge, March 24th; London Season, June 7th; Revival of the 'Playboy', May 27th; Production of Blanco Posnet, August 25th. Told in Press-Cuttings* (Dublin: Privately Printed).

HENN, T. R., 'The Irish Tragedy', *The Harvest of Tragedy* (London: Methuen, 1956; University Paperbacks, 1966).

HEWITT, BARNARD, *History of the Theatre from 1800 to the Present* (New York: Random House, 1970).

HOBSON, BULMER (ed.), *The Gate Theatre, Dublin* (Dublin: The Gate Theatre, 1934).

HOGAN, ROBERT, *After the Irish Renaissance; A Critical History of the Irish Drama Since 'The Plough and the Stars'* (Minneapolis: University of Minnesota Press, 1967; London: Macmillan, 1968).

and JAMES KILROY (eds.), *Lost Plays of the Irish Renaissance* (Newark, Del.: Proscenium Press, 1970).

and MICHAEL J. O'NEILL (eds.), *Joseph Holloway's Abbey Theatre: A Selection from His Unpublished Journal 'Impressions of a Dublin Playgoer'*. With a Preface by Harry T. Moore (Carbondale & Edwardsville: Southern Illinois University Press, 1967).

and MICHAEL J. O'NEILL (eds.), *Joseph Holloway's Irish Theatre*, 3 vols. (Dixon, Calif: Proscenium Press, 1968–70).

HORNSTEIN, LILLIAN HERLANDS (ed.), 'Irish Literary Revival', *The Reader's Companion to World Literature* (New York: Mentor Books, 1956) p. 231.

HOWARTH, HERBERT, *The Irish Writers, 1880–1940: Literature Under Parnell's Star* (London: Rockliff, 1958).

HOWE, P. P., *The Repertory Theatre: A Record and a Criticism* (London: Martin Secker, 1910) chap. 2.

HUBBELL, JAY B. and JOHN O. BEATY, 'Irish Dramatists', *An Introduction to Drama* (New York: Macmillan, 1929) pp. 522–4.

HUDSON, LYNTON, 'The Little Theatre: The Irish Movement', *The Twentieth Century Drama* (London: George G. Harrap, 1946) pp. 37–44.

HUNEKER, JAMES, 'The Celtic Awakening', *The Pathos of Distance: A Book of a Thousand and One Moments* (New York: Charles Scribner's; London: T. Werner Laurie, 1922) pp. 219–44.

'Irish Drama', *The New Funk & Wagnalls Encyclopedia*, vol. XI (New York: Unicorn Publishers, 1950) p. 3894.

JACKSON, HOLBROOK, *All Manner of Folk: Interpretations and Studies* (London: Grant Richards, 1912).

The Eighteen Nineties; A Review of Art and Ideas at the Close of the Nineteenth Century (London: Grant Richards, 1913).

JACQUOT, JEAN (ed.), *Le théâtre moderne; hommes et tendances*

A BIBLIOGRAPHY OF MODERN IRISH DRAMA

(Paris: Éditions du centre national de la recherche scientifique, 1965) pp. 321–36.

JAMESON, STORM, *Modern Drama in Europe* (London: Collins; New York: Harcourt, Brace, 1920).

JONES, HENRY ARTHUR, *The Foundations of a National Drama* (New York: George H. Doran, 1913).

JORDON, JOHN, 'The Irish Theatre: Retrospect and Premonition', *Contemporary Theatre*, ed. John Russell Brown and Bernard Harris. Stratford-upon-Avon Studies No. 4 (London: Edward Arnold, 1962).

JOYCE, JAMES, 'The Day of the Rabblement', *The Genius of the Irish Theatre*, ed. by Sylvan Barnet, Morton Berman and William Burto. Mentor Books (New York: The New American Library, 1960).

The Critical Writings of James Joyce, ed. by Ellsworth Mason and Richard Ellmann (London: Faber & Faber, 1959).

KAIN, RICHARD M., *Dublin in the Age of William Butler Yeats and James Joyce* (Norman: University of Oklahoma Press, 1962; repr. 1967).

KAVANAGH, PETER, *The Irish Theatre: Being A History of the Drama in Ireland from the Earliest Period up to the Present Day* (Tralee, Ireland: Kerryman, 1946).

The Story of the Abbey Theatre, from Its Origins in 1899 to the Present (New York: Devin-Adair, 1950).

KELLY, BLANCHE MARY, *The Voice of the Irish* (New York: Sheed & Ward, 1952).

KENNEDY, DAVID, 'The Drama in Ulster', *The Arts in Ulster; A Symposium*, ed. by Sam Hanna Bell *et al.* (London: Harrap, 1951) pp. 47–68.

KENNEDY, J. M., *English Literature 1880–1905* (London: Stephen Swift, 1912).

KERNODLE, GEORGE, 'Poetic Drama of Ireland and Spain', *Invitation to the Theatre* (New York: Harcourt, Brace, 1967) pp. 229–31.

16

KITCHEN, LAURENCE, *Mid-Century Drama* (London: Faber & Faber, 1960; second edition (rev.), 1962).
Drama in the Sixties; Form and Interpretation (London: Faber & Faber, 1966).

KNIGHT, G. WILSON, *The Golden Labyrinth: A Study of British Drama* (London: Phoenix House, 1962; University Paperbacks, 1965).

KRANS, H. S., *W. B. Yeats and the Irish Literary Revival* (New York: McClure, Phillips, 1904; London: Heinemann, 1905).

KRUTCH, JOSEPH WOOD, 'Synge and the Irish Protest', '*Modernism*' in *Modern Drama; A Definition and an Estimate* (Ithaca, New York: Cornell University Press, 1953; Cornell Paperbacks, 1966) pp. 88–103.

KUNITZ, STANLEY J., *Living Authors: A Book of Biographies*, ed. by Dilly Tante (New York: H. W. Wilson, 1931).
and HOWARD HAYCRAFT (eds.), *Twentieth Century Authors: A Biographical Dictionary of Modern Literature* (New York: H. W. Wilson, 1942).
and HOWARD HAYCRAFT (eds.), *Twentieth Century Authors, First Supplement* (New York: H. W. Wilson, 1955).

LAMM, MARTIN, 'Irish Drama', *Modern Drama*, trans. by K. Elliott (Oxford: Blackwell, 1952; New York: Philosophical Library, 1953) pp. 293–314.

LANE, YOTI, *The Psychology of the Actor* (London: Secker & Warburg, 1959).

LAW, HUGH ALEXANDER, 'Dramatists', *Anglo-Irish Literature*. With a Foreword by A. E. (Dublin: Talbot Press; London: Longmans Green, 1926) pp. 250–71.

LAWSON, JOHN HOWARD, *Theory and Technique of Playwriting* (New York: Hill & Wang, 1960).

LEGOUIS, EMILE and LOUIS CAZAMIAN, 'The Celtic

Revival', *A History of English Literature* (London: J. M. Dent, 1965) pp. 1281–9.

LEWIS, ALLAN, *The Contemporary Theatre; the Significant Playwrights of Our Time.* With a Foreword by John Gassner (New York: Crown Publishers, 1962).

LEWISOHN, LUDWIG, 'The Irish Movement', *The Modern Drama* (New York: B. W. Huebsch; London: Martin Secker, 1916; New York: The Viking Press, 1931).

LONG, WILLIAM J., 'The Celtic Revival', *English Literature: Its History and Its Significance for the Life of the English-Speaking World* (Boston: Ginn, 1964) pp. 610–20.

LONGFORD, EARL OF [EDWARD ARTHUR HENRY PAKEN-HAM], 'The Literary Renaissance', *Encyclopaedia Britannica*, vol. 12 (London: Encyclopaedia Britannica, 1970) pp. 596–7.

Longford Productions: Dublin Gate Souvenir, 1939 (Dublin: Corrigan & Wilson, [1939]).

LUCAS, F. L., *The Drama of Chekov, Synge, Yeats, and Pirandello* (London: Cassell, 1965).

LUMLEY, FREDERICK, *New Trends in 20th Century Drama; A Survey Since Ibsen and Shaw* (London: Barrie & Rockliff, 1967).

LYND, ROBERT, 'Literature and Music', *Home Life in Ireland* (London: Mills & Boon, 1909) pp. 305–17.
Old and New Masters (London: R. Fisher Unwin, 1919).

The Lyric Players 1951–1959 (Belfast: Lyric Players, 1960) [brochure to launch an appeal for financial support].
Lyric Theatre 1951–1968 (Belfast, Lyric Theatre [1968]).

McCANN, SEAN (ed.), *The Story of the Abbey Theatre.* A Four Square Book (London: The New English Library, 1967).

MacDONAGH, THOMAS, *Literature in Ireland; Studies Irish and Anglo-Irish* (Dublin: Talbot Press; New York:

Stokes, 1916; Port Washington, N.Y.: Kennikat Press, 1970).

MACGOWAN, KENNETH and WILLIAM MELNITZ, 'The Irish National Theater', *The Living Stage; A History of the World Theater* (Englewood Cliffs, N.J.: Prentice-Hall, 1955) pp. 419–24.

McHENRY, MARGARET, *The Ulster Theatre in Ireland* (Philadelphia: University of Pennsylvania, 1931).

MACKENNA, STEPHEN, *Journal and Letters*, ed. E. R. Dodds (London: Constable, 1936).

MAC LIAMMÓIR, MICHEÁL, *Theatre in Ireland* (Dublin: Published for the Cultural Relations Committee of Ireland at the Three Candles, 1950; Reprinted with Sequel, 1964).
All for Hecuba; An Irish Theatrical Autobiography (London: Methuen, 1946; Dublin, Progress House, 1961).

MACNAMARA, BRINSLEY, *Abbey Plays, 1899–1948* (Dublin: At the Sign of the Three Candles, [1949]).

MALONE, ANDREW E., *The Irish Drama, 1896–1928* (London: Constable; New York: Charles Scribner's, 1929; New York: Benjamin Blom, 1965).

MALYE, JEAN, *La Littérature Irlandaise contemporaine* (Paris: E. Sansot, 1913).

MARCUS, PHILIP, *Yeats and the Beginnings of the Irish Renaissance* (Ithaca, N.Y.: Cornell University Press, 1971).

MARRIOTT, J. W. 'Irish Dramatists', *Modern Drama* (London: Thomas Nelson, [1934]) pp. 190–203
The Theatre (London: George G. Harrap, 1931).

MATTHEWS, BRANDER, 'Irish Plays and Irish Playwrights', *The Principles of Playmaking and Other Discussions of the Drama* (New York: Scribner's, 1919) pp. 196–213.

MELCHINGER, SIEGFRIED, *The Concise Encyclopedia of Modern Drama* (London: Vision Press, 1970).

MERCIER, VIVIAN, *The Irish Comic Tradition* (Oxford: Clarendon Press, 1962; Oxford University Press Paperbacks, 1969).

and DAVID H. GREENE (eds.), *1000 Years of Irish Prose: The Literary Revival* (New York: Devin-Adair, 1952; Grosset & Dunlap, 1961).

MILLER, ANNA IRENE, 'The National Theatre of Ireland', *The Independent Theatre in Europe, 1887 to the Present* (New York: R. Long & R. R. Smith, 1931; Benjamin Blom, 1966) pp. 255–310.

MILLER, NELLIE BURGET, 'The New Theater of Ireland', *The Living Drama* (New York and London: Century, 1924).

MILLET, FRED B., 'The Irish Drama', *Contemporary British Literature* (New York: Harcourt, Brace, 1944), pp. 59–62.

MONAHAN, MICHAEL, *Nova Hibernia: Irish Poets and Dramatists of Today and Yesterday* (New York: M. Kennerley, 1914).

MONTAGUE, C. E., *Dramatic Values* (London: Methuen, 1911).

MOODY, WILLIAM VAUGHAN and ROBERT MORSS LOVETT, 'The Irish Drama', *A History of English Literature*, eighth edition by Fred B. Millett (New York: Charles Scribner's, 1964) pp. 398–401 and 456–60.

MOORE, ALFRED S., *The Little Theatre* (Belfast: Ulster & Dramatic Art, n.d.).

MOORE, GEORGE, *Hail and Farewell* (London: William Heinemann; New York: Appleton, 1911–14), 3 vols.

MORGAN, A. E., *Tendencies of Modern English Drama* (London: Constable; New York: Charles Scribner's, 1924).

MORRIS, LLOYD R., 'The Drama', *The Celtic Dawn: A Survey of the Renaissance in Ireland 1889–1916* (New York:

Macmillan, 1917; New York: Cooper Square Publishers, 1970) chap iv.

NATHAN, GEORGE JEAN, 'The Contribution of the Irish', *The Entertainment of a Nation* (New York: Alfred A. Knopf, 1942).
(ed.), 'Foreword', *Five Great Modern Irish Plays* (New York: The Modern Library, 1941).

NEVINSON, H. W., *Books and Personalities* (London and New York: John Lane, 1905).

NEWMAN, EVELYN, *The International Note in Contemporary Drama* (New York: Kingsland Press, 1931).

NICOLL, ALLARDYCE, *British Drama* (London: George G. Harrap, 1958).
'The Irish School', *World Drama from Aeschylus to Anouilh* (London: George G. Harrap, 1968) pp. 689–98.

NICSHIUBHLAIGH, MAIRE, *The Splendid Years: Recollections of Maire NicShiubhlaigh, As Told to Edward Kenny*. Foreword by Padraic Colum (Dublin: James Duffy, 1955).

O'CASEY, SEAN, *Blasts and Benedictions*, ed. Ronald Ayling (London: Macmillan, 1967).
Mirror in My House (New York: Macmillan, 1956). Reprinted as *Autobiographies* (London: Macmillan, 1963) [Especially *Inishfallen, Fare Thee Well* and *Rose and Crown*].

O'CONNOR, FRANK, *The Backward Look; A Survey of Irish Literature* (London: Macmillan, 1967). American edition entitled *A Short History of Irish Literature; A Backward Look* (New York: Putnam, 1967; Capricorn Books, 1968).
'The Abbey Theatre', *My Father's Son* (London: Macmillan, 1968).

O'CONNOR, NORREYS JEPHSON, *Changing Ireland: Literary Backgrounds of the Irish Free State, 1889–1922* (Cambridge,

Mass.: Harvard University Press; London: Humphrey Milford, 1924).

O'DONNEL, F[RANK] HUGH, *The Stage Irishmen of the Pseudo-Celtic Drama* (London: John Long, 1904).

O'DRISCOLL, ROBERT (ed.), *Theatre and Nationalism in Twentieth-Century Ireland* (Toronto: University of Toronto Press, 1971).

O HAODHA, MICHEAL, *The Abbey – Then and Now* (Dublin: The Abbey Theatre, 1969).

O'NEILL, JAMES J., *Irish Theatrical History: A Biographical Essay* (Dublin: Browne & Nolan, 1910).

PALMER, JOHN, *The Future of the Theatre* (London: G. Bell, 1913).

PAUL-DUBOIS, L., 'The Literary Awakening', *Contemporary Ireland* (Dublin: Maunsel; New York: Baker & Taylor, 1908) pp. 420–30.

PEACOCK, RONALD, *The Poet in the Theatre* (London: Routledge, 1946; New York: Hill & Wang, 1960).

PELLIZI, CAMILLO, 'In Ireland', *English Drama; The Last Great Phase*. Trans. by Rowan Williams (London: Macmillan, 1935) chap vi.

PERRY, HENRY TEN EYCK, *Masters of Dramatic Comedy and Their Social Themes* (Cambridge, Mass.: Harvard University Press, 1939; London: Oxford University Press, 1940; Port Washington, N.Y.: Kennikat Press, 1968) pp. 363–6.

POGSON, REX, *Miss Horniman and the Gaiety Theatre, Manchester* (London: Rockliff, 1952).

POWER, PATRICK C., *A Literary History of Ireland* (Cork: Mercier Press, 1969).

PRICE, ALAN, *Synge and Anglo-Irish Drama* (London: Methuen, 1961).

PRIOR, MOODY E., *The Language of Tragedy* (New York:

Columbia University Press, 1947; Bloomington and London: Indiana University Press, 1966).

PRITCHETT, V. S., *Dublin: A Portrait* (London: The Bodley Head, 1967).

RAFROIDI, PATRICK, RAYMONDE POPOT and WILLIAM PARKER (eds.), *Aspects of the Irish Theatre* (Lille: Université de Lille, 1972).

REYNOLDS, ERNEST, 'Yeats, Synge, and the Irish School', *Modern English Drama; A Survey of the Theatre from 1900*. With a Foreword by Allardyce Nicoll (London: George G. Harrap, 1949; Norman, Okl.: University of Oklahoma Press, 1951) pp. 87–97.

RIVOALLAN, ANATOLE, *Littérature irlandaise contemporaien* (Paris: Hachette, 1939) chap. 6.

ROBINSON, LENNOX (ed.), *The Irish Theatre: Lectures Delivered During the Abbey Theatre Festival Held in Dublin in August 1938* (London: Macmillan, 1939; New York: Haskell House, 1971).
   Curtain Up: An Autobiography (London: Michael Joseph, 1942).
   Pictures in a Theatre; A Conversation Piece (Dublin: The Abbey Theatre, [1947]).
   Ireland's Abbey Theatre; A History 1899–1951 (London: Sidgwick & Jackson, 1951; Port Washington, N.Y.: Kennikat Press, 1968).

ROWE, KENNETH THORPE, *Write That Play* (New York and London: Funk & Wagnalls, 1939; New York: Funk & Wagnalls, 1968) pp. 61–122.

RUSSELL, CARO MAE GREEN, 'Ireland', *Modern Plays and Playwrights* (Chapel Hill, N.C.: University of North Carolina Press, 1936).

RUSSELL, DIARMUID, 'Introduction', *The Portable Irish Reader* (New York: The Viking Press, 1946) pp. xi–xxx.

RYAN, W. P., 'Ireland at the Play', *The Pope's Green Island* (London: Nisbet, 1912) chap. xxiv.

SADDLEMYER, ANN (ed.), *Theatre Business, Management of Men. The Letters of the First Abbey Theatre Directors* (New York: New York Public Library, 1971).

SAHAL, N., *Sixty Years of Realistic Irish Drama (1900–1960)* (Bombay: Macmillan, 1971).

SAMPSON GEORGE, 'Anglo-Irish Literature', *The Concise Cambridge History of English Literature* (Cambridge: Cambridge University Press, 1961) pp. 887–909.

SAMACHSON, DOROTHY & JOSEPH, 'Dublin, 1907', *The Dramatic Story of the Theatre* (London: Abelard-Schuman, 1955) pp. 128–33.

SAUL, GEORGE BRANDON (ed.), 'Introduction', *Age of Yeats: The Golden Age of Irish Literature* (New York: Dell, 1964).

SCOTT-JAMES, R. A., 'The Irish Literary Movement', *Fifty Years of English Literature 1900–1950. With a Postscript —1951 to 1955* (London: Longmans, 1956) pp. 89–98.

SETTERQUIST, JAN, *Ibsen and the Beginnings of Anglo-Irish Drama.* Upsala Irish Studies (Dublin: Hodges, Figgis, 1952).

SHANK, THEODORE J. (ed.), 'Irish Drama' *A Digest of 500 Plays; Plot Outlines and Production Notes* (New York: Collier Books; London: Collier-Macmillan, 1963) pp. 411–18.

SHARP, R. FARQUHARSON, 'The Dublin Theatres', *A Short History of the English Stage from Its Beginnings to the Summer of the Year 1908* (New York: Walter Scott, 1909) chap. xx.

SHAW, BERNARD, *A Note on the Irish Theatre by Theodore Roosevelt and an 'Interview' on the Irish Players in America by George Bernard Shaw* (New York: Mitchell Kennerly, 1912).

The Matter with Ireland, ed. with an Introduction by David H. Greene and Dan H. Laurence (London: Rupert Hart-Davis, 1962).

SHIPLEY, JOSEPH T., *Guide to Great Plays* (Washington: Public Affairs Press, 1956).

SHORT, ERNEST, *Theatrical Cavalcade* (London: Eyre & Spottiswoode, 1942; The Woman's Book Club, 1943) pp. 205–10.

'The Irish Players', *Sixty Years of Theatre* (London: Eyre & Spottiswoode, 1951) pp. 374–8.

SIMPSON, ALAN, *Beckett and Behan and a Theatre in Dublin* (London: Routledge & Kegan Paul, 1962).

SKELTON, ROBIN and DAVID R. CLARK (eds.), *Irish Renaissance* (Dublin: The Dolmen Press, 1959).

and ANN SADDLEMYER (eds.), *The World of W. B. Yeats: Essays in Perspective* (Victoria, B.C.: Published for the University of Victoria by the Adelphi Bookshop Ltd., 1965).

SOBEL, BERNARD (ed.), *The New Theatre Handbook and Digest of Plays*. Preface by George Freedley (New York: Crown Publishers, 1959).

SPEAIGHT, ROBERT, *Drama Since 1939* (London: Longmans, Green for the British Council, 1947) pp. 25–8.

SPINNER, KASPAR, *Die Alte Dame Sagt: Nein! Drei Irische Dramatiker: Lennox Robinson – Sean O'Casey – Denis Johnston*. Swiss Studies in English (Berne: Francke Verlag, 1961).

SPRINCHORN, EVERT (ed.), *20th-Century Plays in Synopsis* (New York: Thomas Y. Crowell, 1965).

STYAN, J. L., *The Elements of Drama* (Cambridge: Cambridge University Press, 1960).

The Dark Comedy; The Development of Modern Comic Tragedy (Cambridge: Cambridge University Press, 1968).

The Dramatic Experience; A Guide to the Reading of Plays (Cambridge: Cambridge University Press, 1965).

SYNGE, J. M., *Collected Works*, vol. 2: *Prose*, ed. Alan Price (London: Oxford University Press, 1966).

TAYLOR, ESTELLA RUTH, *The Modern Irish Writers; Cross Currents of Criticism* (Lawrence: University of Kansas Press, 1954; New York: Greenwood Press, 1969).

TINDALL, WILLIAM YORK, *Forces in Modern British Literature 1885–1956*. Vintage Books (New York: Random House, 1956) pp. 65–74.

TREWIN, J. C., *The English Theatre* (London: Paul Elek, 1948). *Dramatists of Today* (London: Staples Press, 1953).

TYNAN, KATHARINE, *Twenty-Five Years: Reminiscences* (London: John Murray, 1913).

USSHER, PERCY A., *Three Great Irishmen: Shaw, Yeats, Joyce* (London: Victor Gollancz, 1952).

VAN DOREN, CARL and MARK VAN DOREN, 'Irish Literature: Drama', *American and British Literature Since 1890* (New York: Appleton-Century-Crofts, 1967) pp. 324–40.

VERNON, FRANK, *The Twentieth-Century Theatre* (London: George G. Harrap, 1924).

WALBROOK, H. M., *Nights at the Play* (London: W. J. Ham-Smith, 1911).

WALKLEY, A. B., 'The Irish National Theatre', *Drama and Life* (London: Methuen, 1907; New York: Brentano's, 1908; Freeport, N.Y.: Books for Libraries Press, 1967) pp. 309–15.

WARD, A. C., 'The Irish Theatre', *Twentieth-Century English Literature 1901–1960* (London: Methuen, 1966) pp. 110–17.

WAUCHOPE, A. G., *The New Irish Drama* (Columbia, S.C.: University of South Carolina Press, 1919).

WEYGANDT, CORNELIUS, *Irish Plays and Playwrights* (London: Constable; Boston and New York: Houghton Mifflin, 1913; Port Washington, N.Y.: Kennikat Press, 1966).

WILLIAMS, HAROLD, 'The Irish Literary Theatre' and 'The Irish Playwrights', *Modern English Writers: Being a Study of Imaginative Literature 1890–1914* (London: Sidgwick & Jackson, 1925; Port Washington, N.Y.: Kennikat Press, 1970) pp. 193–6 and 197–220 respectively.

WILLIAMS, RAYMOND, *Drama from Ibsen to Brecht* (London: Chatto & Windus, 1968).

WILLIAMSON, AUDREY, 'Irish Stew and Russian Salad', *Theatre of Two Decades* (London: Rockliff, 1951) chap. xi.

YEATS, W. B., *Dramatis Personae* (London: Macmillan, 1936,). Reprinted in *Autobiographies* (London: Macmillan, 1955). (ed.), *Samhain* (London: Frank Cass, 1970).
The Cutting of an Agate (London and New York: Macmillan, 1912). Reprinted in *Essays* (London: Macmillan, 1924); and in *Essays and Introductions* (London: Macmillan, 1961).
'The Irish Dramatic Movement', *Plays and Controversies* (London: Macmillan, 1923) pp. 1–218.
'A Note on National Drama', *Literary Ideals in Ireland* (London: Fisher Unwin, 1899).
'Advice to Playwrights Who are Sending Plays to the Abbey, Dublin', *The Genius of the Irish Theater*, ed. by Sylvan Barnet, Morton Berman, and William Burto. Mentor Books (New York: The New American Library, 1960).
The Irish National Theatre (Rome: Reale Accademia d'Italia, 1935).
'The Celtic Element in Literature', *Essays* (London: Macmillan, 1924) pp. 213–31. Reprinted in *Essays and Introductions* (London: Macmillan, 1961) pp. 173–89.

'The Literary Movement in Ireland', *Ideals in Ireland*, ed. by Lady Gregory (London: Unicorn, 1901) pp. 87–102.

(ed.), *Beltaine; The Organ of the Irish Literary Theatre* (London: Frank Cass, 1970).

Explorations (London: Macmillan, 1962).

Essays (New York: Macmillan, 1924).

Autobiographies (London: Macmillan, 1955).

YOUNG, ELLA, *Flowering Dusk; Things Remembered Accurately and Inaccurately* (New York: Longmans, Green, 1945).

YOUNG, STARK, *The Flower in Drama* (New York: Scribner's, 1955).

3. Periodicals

'The Abbey', *Newsweek* (Dayton, Ohio), LXVIII, No. 5 (1 Aug 1966) 82.

'The Abbey Theatre', *Theatre Arts Monthly* (N.Y.), XVI, No. 9 (Sep 1932) 692, 695.

'The Abbey Theatre', *The Irish Times* (Dublin) (28 July 1944) p. 3.

'The Abbey Theatre: Its Origins and Accomplishments', *The Times* (London) (17 Mar 1913): Irish Number p. 15.

'The Abbey Theatre Subsidy', *The Literary Digest* (N.Y.), LXXXVI (12 Sep 1925) 29-30.

'Abbey's New Policy', *The Evening Herald* (Dublin) (13 Aug 1935) p. 7. Reprinted in *The Literary Digest* (N.Y.) (1 June 1935) 24.

'Acting of the Irish Players', *The New York Times* (26 Nov 1911) p. 3.

ADAMS, J. DONALD, 'The Irish Dramatic Movement', *The Harvard Monthly* (Cambridge, Mass.) (Nov 1911) 44-8.

ALLDRIDGE, JOHN, 'What's Wrong with the Abbey?' *Irish Digest* (Dublin), XXIX, No. 4 (Feb 1948) 17-19. Condensed from *Manchester Evening News*.

ALLEN, PERCY, 'The Theatre in Ulster', *The Daily Telegraph* (London) (25 Mar 1926). Reprinted in *The Living Age* (Boston), CCCXXIX (29 May 1926) 467-9.

'The Art of the Irish Players', *Everybody's Magazine* (N.Y.), XXVI (Feb 1912) 231–40.

'Au Revoir to the Abbey Theatre', *The Sunday Times* (London) (25 Jan 1959) p. 9.

AYLING, RONALD, 'W. B. Yeats on Plays and Players', *Modern Drama* (Lawrence, Kansas), IX, No. 1 (May 1966) 1–10.

BAUGHAN, E. A., 'The Irish Players', *The Daily News and Leader* (London) (14 July 1913) p. 6.

BEHAN, D., 'Posterity and After', *The Spectator* (London), CCIV (29 Apr 1960) 619–20.

BENNETT, JAMES O'DONNELL, 'Lessons of the Abbey Theatre Engagement', *Record Herald* (Chicago) (3 Mar 1912) Part 7, p. 1.

BENTLEY, ERIC, 'World Theatre: 1900–1950', *Theatre Arts* (N.Y.), XXXIII (Dec 1949) 22–7.
'Irish Theatre: Splendeurs et Misères', *Poetry* (Chicago), LXXIX, No. 4 (Jan 1952) 216–32. Reprinted in *In Search of Theater* (New York: Vintage Books, 1953) pp. 315–21.

BEWLEY, CHARLES, 'The Irish National Theatre', *The Dublin Review*, CLII, No. 304 (Jan 1913) 132–44. Reprinted in *The Living Age* (Boston), CCLXXVI (15 Feb 1913) 410–18.

BIRMINGHAM, GEORGE A., 'The Literary Movement in Ireland', *Fortnightly Review* (London and New York), LXXXII, New Series (Dec 1907) 947–57.

BISSING, TOSKA, 'Dublin Gate Theatre Productions', *Theatre Arts* (N.Y.), XXV, No. 1 (Jan 1941) 49–52.

BLAKE, WARREN BARTON, 'Irish Plays and Players', *Independent* (N.Y.), LXXIV (6 Mar 1913) 515–19.

Boston Evening Transcript. [An important series of articles appeared in this periodical from 19 Sep to 20 Oct 1911, while the Abbey Players were in the United States.]

BOWEN, EVELYN, 'The Theatre: Dublin', *The Bell* (Dublin), V, No. 3 (1942) 236–8.

BOYD, ERNEST A., 'The Irish National Theatre; A Criticism', *The Irish Times* (Dublin) (27 Dec 1912) p. 5.
'The Abbey Theatre', *The Irish Review* (Dublin), II, No. 24 (Feb 1913) 628–34.
'Le Théâtre irlandais', *Revue de Paris*, V (1 Sep 1913) 191–205.

BRERETON-BARRY, R., 'The Need for a State Theatre', *The Irish Statesman* (Dublin), III, No. 7 (25 Oct 1924) 210–12.

BRIDGES-ADAMS, W., 'A National Theatre', *Drama* (London), No. 51 (Winter 1958) 27–30.

BROMAGE, MARY COGAN, 'Literature of Ireland Today', *South Atlantic Quarterly* (Durham, N.C.), XLII, No. 1 (Jan 1943) 27–37.

BROOKS, SYDNEY, 'The Irish Peasant As A Dramatic Issue', *Harper's Weekly* (N.Y.), LI (9 Mar 1907) 344.

BROSNAN, GERALD, 'Dublin's Abbey – the Immortal Theatre', *Theatre Arts* (N.Y.), XXXV, No. 10 (Oct 1951) 36–7.

BURROWES, WESLEY, 'Writers Are Not Encouraged', *The Irish Times* (Dublin) (18 Mar 1968) p. 10.

CARROLL, DONALD, 'Contemporary Irish Theatre', *Drama* (London), No. 66 (Autumn 1962) 34–6.

CARROLL, PAUL VINCENT, 'Can the Abbey Theatre Be Restored?' *Theatre Arts* (N.Y.), XXXVI, No. 1 (Jan 1952) 18–19, 79.

CARTER, WILLIAM, 'Lament for the Province without Playwrights', *Ireland Today*, I, No. 7 (1936) 68–9.

CASWELL, ROBERT W., 'Unity and the Irish Theatre', *Studies; An Irish Quarterly Review* (Dublin), XLIX, No. 193 (Spring 1960) 63–7.

31

CHAMBERS, E. K., 'Drama: The Experiments of Mr Yeats', *The Academy and Literature* (London), LXIV (9 May 1903) 465–6. [On plays given by the Irish National Theatre Society at the Queen's Gate Hall]. See reply by Yeats, 'Irish Plays and Players', LXIV (16 May 1903) 495. [Letter to the Editor.]

CHANEL, 'The Deserted Abbey', *The Leader* (Dublin), XII, No. 10 (28 Apr 1906) 151–2.

CLARK, JAMES M., 'The Irish Literary Movement', *Englische Studien* (Leipzig), IL (July 1915) 50–98.

CLARKE, MICHAEL, 'The Abbey Theatre', *The Irish Times* (Dublin) (11 Aug 1944) p. 3 [Letter to the Editor.]

COFFEY, BRIAN, 'In Dublin', *The Commonweal* (N.Y.), XLVI (3 Oct 1947) 597–8.

COHEN, HELEN LOUISE, 'The Irish National Theatre', *Scholastic* (Pittsburgh), XXIV (17 Mar 1934) 7–8.

COLE, ALAN, 'The Gate Influence on Dublin Theatre', *The Dublin Magazine*, XXIX, No. 3 (July–Sep 1953) 6–14.

COLGAN, GERALD, 'Threadbare Harlequin', *Plays and Players* (London), X, No. 5 (Feb 1963) 20–4.
'Dublin 1', *Plays and Players* (London), XVIII, No. 8 (May 1971) 52–3.

COLUM, PADRAIC, 'The Irish Literary Movement', *The Forum* (N.Y. and London), LIII (Jan 1915) 133–48.
'Youngest Ireland', *The Seven Arts Magazine* (N.Y.), II, No. 11 (Sep 1917) 608–23.
'The Abbey Theatre Comes of Age', *Theatre Arts Monthly* (N.Y.), X, No. 9 (Sep 1926) 580–4.
'Ibsen in Irish Writing', *Irish Writing* (Cork), No. 7 (Feb 1949) 66–70.
'Theatre: Dublin', *Theatre Arts* (N.Y.), XLIV, No. 2 (Feb 1960) 24–5.

COOPER, BRYAN, 'The Drama in Ireland', *The Irish Review* (Dublin), III (May 1913) 140–3.

PERIODICALS

COXE, LOUIS, 'Letter from Dublin', *The Nation* (N.Y.), CXC, No. 13 (26 Mar 1960) 282.

CRAWFORD, MARY CAROLINE, 'The Irish Players', *The Theatre* (N.Y.), (November 1911) 157–8.

CRONIN, ANTHONY, 'Theatre', *The Bell* (Dublin), XVII, No. 6 (1951) 56–8. [On Belfast Arts Theatre visit to Dublin.]

CUSACK, CYRIL, 'In Terms of Theatre', *Iris Hibernia* (Fribourg, Switzerland), IV, No. 3 (1960) 20–6.

DAVIE, DONALD, 'The Dublin Theatre Festival', *The Twentieth Century* (London), CLXII (July 1957) 71–3,

DE BLAGHD, EARNAN, 'Amharclann na Mainistreach', *Iris Hibernia* (Fribourg, Switzerland), IV, No. 3 (1960) 43–5.

'The Decadence of the Abbey', *Saturday Herald* (Dublin), (19 July 1913), Magazine Page.

DE PAOR, SEORAM, 'The Ulster Literary Theatre', *Ulad: A Literary and Critical Magazine* (Balfast), I, No. 4 (Sep 1905) 5–10.

DESMOND, SHAW, 'The Irish Renaissance', *The Outlook* (N.Y.), CXXXVIII (15 Oct 1924) 247–9.

'De Valera As Play Censor', *The Manchester Guardian Weekly*, XXX, No. 15 (13 Apr 1934) 296.

DIGGES, DUDLEY, 'A Theatre Was Made', *Irish Digest* (Dublin), IV, No. 4 (Oct 1939) 11–14. Condensed from *The Recorder; Bulletin of the American Irish Historical Society* (N.Y.).

DONN, UILLIAM, 'The Ulster Literary Theatre', *Ulad; A Literary and Critical Magazine* (Belfast), I, No. 1 (Nov 1904) 7–8.

DONOGHUE, DENIS, 'Irish Writing', *Month*, XVII (1957) 180–185.

'Dublin Letter', *The Hudson' Review*, XIII (Winter 1960-1) 579–85

A BIBLIOGRAPHY OF MODERN IRISH DRAMA

'Drama', *The Nation* (N.Y.), XCIII (30 Nov 1911) 528–9.

DUFFUS, R. L., 'Dublin – Story of Two Cities. St. Patrick's Day Finds the Old Poetry of the City Co-Existing with a New Vitality', *The New York Times Magazine* (17 Mar 1957) 28, 39, 41.

DUKES, ASHLEY, 'The Irish Scene: Dublin Plays and Play-houses', *Theatre Arts Monthly* (N.Y.), XIV, No. 5 (May 1930) 378–84.

'Dull Gaelic Plough', *Newsweek* (Dayton, Ohio), XXX, No. 21 (24 Nov 1947) 84.

DUNSANY, LORD, 'Romance and the Modern Stage', *National Review* (London), LVII (July 1911) 827–35.
'Some Irish Writers Whom I have Known', *Irish Writing* (Cork), Nos. 20–1 (Nov 1952) 78–82.

EBERHART, RICHARD, 'Memory of Meeting Yeats, AE. Gogarty, James Stephens', *The Literary Review*, I (1957), 51–6.

ERVINE, ST JOHN G., 'The Irish Dramatist and the Irish People', *The Forum* (N.Y.), LI (June 1914) 940–8.

EVERSON, IDA G., 'Young Lennox Robinson and the Abbey Theatre's First American Tour (1911–1912)', *Modern Drama* (Lawrence, Kansas), IX, No. 1 (May 1966) 74–89.

FALLON, GABRIEL, 'More About a Catholic Theatre', *Irish Rosary* (Dublin), XXXIX, No. 11 (Nov 1935) 810–14.
'The Ageing Abbey', *The Irish Monthly* (Dublin), LXVI, No. 778 (Apr 1938) 265–72; LXVI, No. 779 (May 1938) 339–44.
'Tribute to the Fays', *The Irish Monthly* (Dublin), LXXIII (Jan 1945) 18–24.
'Maritain Was Wrong', *The Commonweal* (N.Y.), LII (26 May 1950) 175–6.
'Why Is There No Irish Claudel or Mauriac?' *Evening Press* (Dublin) (5 Feb 1955) p. 5.

'The Future of the Irish Theatre', *Studies: An Irish Quarterly Review* (Dublin), XLIV (Spring 1955) 92–100.

'Dublin Letter', *America* (N.Y.), XCVIII, No. 2 (12 Oct 1957) 46–7.

'All This and the Abbey Too', *Studies: An Irish Quarterly Review* (Dublin), XLVIII, No. 192 (Winter 1959) 434–42.

'The Abbey Theatre Today', *Iris Hibernia* (Fribourg, Switzerland), IV, No. 3 (1960) 46–54.

'Dublin's Fourth Theatre Festival', *Modern Drama* (Lawrence, Kansas), V, No. 1 (May 1962) 21–6.

FARRELL, JAMES T., 'The Irish Cultural Renaissance in the Last Century', *Irish Writing* (Cork), No. 25 (Dec 1935) 50–3.

FARRELL, MICHAEL, 'Drama in Ulster Now', *The Bell* (Dublin), II, No. 4 (1941) 82–8.

FAY, FRANK J., 'The Irish Literary Theatre', *The United Irishman* (Dublin), V, No. 114 (4 May 1901).

'An Irish National Theatre', *The United Irishman* (Dublin), V, No. 115 (11 May 1901); and V, No. 116 (18 May 1901).

'*Samhain*', *The United Irishman* (Dublin), VI, No. 139 (26 Oct 1901).

'The Irish Literary Theatre', *The United Irishman* (Dublin), VI, No. 140 (2 Nov 1901).

'The Irish Literary Theatre', *The United Irishman* (Dublin), VI, No. 143 (23 Nov 1901).

FAY, GERARD, 'The Irish Theatre', *Drama* (London), No. 84 (Spring 1967) 33–5.

FINN, SEAMUS, 'The Abbey Theatre', *The Irish Times* (Dublin) (29 July 1944) p. 3. [Letter to the Editor.]

FINNIAN, 'Gael-Linn agus an Dramaiocht', *Iris Hibernia* (Fribourg, Switzerland), IV, No. 3 (1960) 58–62.

FITZ-SIMON, CHRISTOPHER, 'The Theatre in Dublin', *Modern Drama* (Lawrence, Kansas), II, No. 3 (Dec 1959) 289–94.

FORD, MARY K., 'Is the Celtic Revival Distinctly Irish?' *North American Review* (N.Y.), CLXXXIII, No. 601 (Oct 1906) 771-5.

'Forty Years of Irish Drama', *The Times Literary Supplement* (London) (13 Apr 1940) 182, 186.

FOX, R. M., 'Realism in Irish Drama', *The Irish Statesman* (Dublin), X (23 June 1928) 310-12.

'The Theatre Goes on In Ireland', *Theatre Arts* (N.Y.), XXIV, No. 11 (Nov 1940) 783-6.

'Ups and Downs in the Irish Theatre', *Theatre Arts* (N.Y.), XXV, No. 5 (May 1941) 353-8.

'What Next in Irish Drama?' *Theatre Arts* (N.Y.), XXVI, No. 4 (Apr 1942) 245-9.

'Wild Riders of Irish Drama', *Theatre Arts* (N.Y.), XXVIII, No. 5 (May 1944) 301-4.

'Irish Theatre', *Theatre Arts* (N.Y.), XXIX, No. 5 (May 1945) 286-93.

'Irish Drama in War and Peace', *Theatre Arts* (N.Y.), XXX, No. 4 (Apr 1946) 231-5.

'Twilight over Irish Drama', *Theatre Arts* (N.Y.), XXX, No. 12 (Dec 1946) 706-8.

'The Theatre in Eire', *Theatre Arts* (N.Y.), XXXI, No. 11 (Nov 1947) 30.

'Irish Drama Knocks at the Door', *Life and Letters* (London), LXI, No. 140 (Apr 1949) 16-21.

'Same Program, Fifty Years Later', *The American Mercury*, LXXXI (July 1955) 43-4.

GASSNER, JOHN, 'The Theatre Arts', *The Forum* (Philadelphia), CIX (Apr 1948) 212-14.

GILL, MICHAEL J., 'Neo-Paganism and the Stage', *The New Ireland Review* (Dublin), XXVII (May 1907) 179-87.

GRAY, KEN, 'T. E. on the Abbey', *The Irish Times* (Dublin) (21 July 1966) p. 8.

GREGORY, LADY ISABELLA AUGUSTA, 'The Coming of

the Irish Players', *Collier's Magazine* (Springfield, O.), XLVIII (21 Oct 1911) 15–24.

'The Irish Theatre and the People', *Yale Review* (New Haven, Conn.), I, No. 2 (Jan 1912) 188–91.

GUNNELL, DORIS, 'Le nouveau Theatre irlandais', *La Revue* (Paris) (1 Jan 1912) 91.

GUNNING, G. HAMILTON, 'The Decline of Abbey Theatre Drama', *The Irish Review* (Dublin), I, No. 12 (Feb 1912) 606–9.

GUTHRIE, TYRONE, 'Closeup of Ireland's Basic Problem', *New York Times Magazine* (19 Jan 1964) 22, 24, 26.

GWYNN, STEPHEN, 'The Irish Literary Theatre and Its Affinities', *Fortnightly Review* (London), LXXVI, New Series LXX (Dec 1901) 1050–62.

'An Uncommercial Theatre', *Fortnightly Review* (London), LXXII, New Series (Sep 1902) 1044–54.

'Poetry and the Stage', *Fortnightly Review* (London and N.Y.), LXXXV, New Series (Feb 1909) 337–51.

HAMILTON, CLAYTON, 'The Irish National Theatre', *The Bookman* (N.Y.), XXXIV, No. 5 (Jan 1912) 508–16. Reprinted in *Studies in Stagecraft* (New York: Henry Holt, 1914).

'The Players', *Everybody's Magazine* (N.Y.), XXVIII (May 1913) 678–80.

HANNAY, J. O., 'The Stage Irishman: His Origin and Development', *The Irish Times* (Dublin) (8 Feb 1912) p. 7. [Lecture at the Theatre of the Royal Dublin Society.]

HAYES, J. J., 'The Little Theatre Movement in Ireland', *The Drama Magazine* (Chicago), XVI (Apr 1926) 261–2.

'Who Will Go To Ireland for Aonach Tailteann?' *Theatre Arts Monthly* (N.Y.), XV, No. 1 (Jan 1931) 78–80.

'The Irish Scene', *Theatre Arts Monthly* (N.Y.), XVI, No. 11 (Nov 1932) 922–6.

'Theatre in Ireland', *Christian Science Monitor Magazine* (Boston) (15 Mar 1947) 19.

HENDERSON, W. A., 'Three Centuries of the Stage Literature of Ireland', *New Ireland Review* (Dublin) (May 1897) 168–78.

HEWES HENRY, 'Broadway Postscript: Dublin', *The Saturday Review* (N.Y.), XL (18 May 1957) 34–5.
'Broadway Postscript: The September Rising', *The Saturday Review* (N.Y.), XLIII (10 Sep 1960) 33, 36.

'A History of the Abbey', *Sunday Independent* (Dublin), XLIV, No. 4 (23 Jan 1949) 3.

HOARE, JOHN EDWARD, 'Ireland's National Drama', *North American Review* (N.Y.), CXCIV (Oct 1911) 566–75.

HOGAN, ROBERT, 'Dublin: The Summer Season and the Theatre Festival, 1967', *Drama Survey*, VI (Spring 1968) 315–23.
'The Year in Review: 1967. Theatre', *University Review* (Dublin), V (1968) 103–12.

'How We Spoiled the Irish Actors', *The Literary Digest* (N.Y.), XLV, No. 2 (13 July 1912) 63.

HUGHES, CATHARINE, 'Theatre in Dublin', *The Nation* (N.Y.), CCIX, No. 18 (24 Nov 1969) 579–81.

'In the Public View: The Irish Players', *Philadelphia Record* (22 Oct 1912).

IRIAL, 'Has the Irish Literary Theatre Failed?' *The United Irishman* (Dublin), VI, No. 141 (9 Nov 1901) 3.

'The Irish Literary Theatre in New York', *The Gael* (N.Y.), (June 1900) 189–90.

'Irish National Theatre', *The Gael* (N.Y.) (Apr 1904) 139.

'The Irish Play of Today', *The Outlook* (N.Y.), IC (4 Nov 1911) 561–3.

'The Irish Players', *The Nation* (N.Y.), XCIII (30 Nov 1911) 528–9.

'The Irish Players in New York', *The Outlook* (N.Y.), IC (2 Dec 1911) 801.

'Irish Plays and Players', *The Outlook* (N.Y.), IIC (29 July 1911) 704.

'The Irish Theatre', *Literary World* (London) (5 June 1913) 182–3.

'The Irish Theatre as an Exponent of the Irish People', *Review of Reviews* (N.Y.), XLV (Mar 1912) 356–7.

JOHNSTON, DENIS, 'Humor – Hibernian Style', *The New York Times* (5 Feb 1961), Drama Section, p. 3.

KELLEHER, JOHN V., 'Irish Literature Today', *Atlantic Monthly* (Boston), CLXXV (Mar 1945) 70–6.

KELLY, SEAMUS, 'Where Motley is Worn', *The Spectator* (London), CXCVI (20 Apr 1956) 538–40.
'Dublin', *Holiday* (Philadelphia, Pa.), XIX, No. 1 (Jan 1956) 38–43.
'Bridgehead Revisited', *The Spectator* (London), CCIV (29 Apr 1960) 626–8.

KENNEDY, DAVID, 'The Theatre in Ulster, 1944–53', *Rann*, No. 20 (1953) 39–42.
'The Ulster Region and the Theatre', *Lagan*, II, No. 1 (1946) 51–6. Reprinted as 'Ulster Theatre' in *Irish Bookman*, I (1947) 33–9.

KENNY, M., 'The Plays of the "Irish" Players', *America* (N.Y.), VI, No. 4 (4 Nov 1911) 78–9.

KEOHLER, THOMAS, 'The Irish National Theatre', *Dana* (Dublin), No. 10 (Feb 1905) 319–20; No. 11 (Mar 1905) 351–2.

KILROY, THOMAS, 'Groundwork for an Irish Theatre', *Studies; An Irish Quarterly Review* (Dublin), XLVIII, No. 190 (Summer 1959) 192–8.

LAWRENCE, W. J., 'Dublin As A Play-Producing Centre,' *The Weekly Freeman* (Dublin), XCI (14 Dec 1907) 25.

'The Abbey Theatre: Its History and Mystery', *The Weekly Freeman* (Dublin), XCVI (7 Dec 1912) 11–12.

'League Discovers the Irish Players', *New York Press* (4 Dec 1911).

LETTS, WINIFRED, 'The Fays at the Abbey Theatre', *The Fortnightly* (London), No. 978, New Series (June 1948) 420–3.

'Young Days at the Abbey Theatre', *Irish Writing* (Cork), No. 61 (Sep 1951) 43–6.

LEWIS-CROSBY, J. E. C., 'CEMA and the Professional Theatre', *Threshold*, III, No. 2 (1959) 21–3.

'A Lively Discussion over the "Irish Plays"', *Boston Sunday Post* (8 Oct 1911) 37.

LOUDAN, JACK, 'Ulster and a Subsidised Theatre', *Lagan*, II, No. 1 (1946) 57–62.

MACARDLE, DOROTHY, 'Experiment in Ireland', *Theatre Arts Monthly* (N.Y.), XVIII, No. 2 (Feb 1934) 124–32.

McBRIEN, PETER, 'Dramatic Ideals of Today', *Studies; An Irish Quarterly Review* (Dublin), XI, No. 42 (June 1922) 235–42.

McCAFFREY, LAWRENCE J., 'Trends in Post-Revolutionary Irish Literature', *College English*, XVIII (1956) 26–30.

MACDONAGH, JOHN, 'Acting in Dublin', *The Commonweal* (N.Y.), X (19 June 1929) 185–6.

McHUGH, ROGER, 'Yeats, Synge and the Abbey Theatre', *Studies; An Irish Quarterly Review* (Dublin), XLI, Nos. 163–4 (Sep–Dec 1952) 333–40.

'Drama in Ireland Today', *Iris Hibernia* (Fribourg, Switzerland), IV, No. 3 (1960) 40–2.

McNEILL, JANET, *et al.*, 'Belfast Theatre Controversy', *Threshold*, III, No. 2 (1959) 24–8.

MacNulty, Edward, 'The Adoration of the Peasant', *The New Age* (London), IX, No. 18 (31 Aug 1911) 416.

Malone, Andrew E., 'The Decline of the Irish Drama', *The Nineteenth Century and After* (London), XCVII, No. 578 (Apr 1925) 578–88.

'The Coming of Age of the Irish Drama', *The Dublin Review*, CLXXXI, No. 362 (July 1927) 101–14.

'The Drama in Ireland', *The Catholic World* (N.Y.), CXXVI (Oct 1927) 109–10.

'The Abbey Theatre Season', *The Dublin Magazine*, II, No. 4 (Oct–Dec 1927) 30–8.

'Ireland', *The Drama Magazine* (Chicago), XXI (Dec 1930) 19, 24.

'The Irish Theatre in 1933', *The Dublin Magazine*, IX, No. 3 (July–Sep 1934) 45–54.

Manning, Mary, 'In Dublin Today', *The Saturday Review of Literature* (N.Y.), VI (17 May 1930) 1048–50.

Martin, Augustine, 'Inherited Dissent: The Dilemma of the Irish Writer', *Studies; An Irish Quarterly Review* (Dublin), LIV, No. 213 (Spring 1965) 1–20.

Martyn, Edward, 'A Comparison between Irish and English Audiences', *Beltaine* (London) No. 2 (February 1900) 11–13.

'A Plea for a National Theatre in Ireland', *Samhain* (Dublin) (Oct 1901) 14–15.

'A Plea for the Revival of the Irish Literary Theatre', *The Irish Review* (Dublin), IV, No. 38 (Apr 1914) 79–84.

Masefield, John, 'The Irish National Theatre', *Manchester Guardian* (2 Jan 1905) p. 3.

Mennloch, Walter, 'Dramatic Values', *The Irish Review* (Dublin), I, No. 7 (Sep 1911) 325–9.

Mercier, Vivian, 'The Dublin Tradition', *The New Republic* (N.Y.), CXXXV, No. 6 (6 Aug 1956) 21–2.

MILLIGAN, ALICE, 'Literary Theatre Week in Dublin', *The Gael* (N.Y.) (Dec 1901) 363–4.

MONTGOMERY, K. L., 'Some Writers of the Celtic Renaissance', *Fortnightly Review* (London and N.Y.), XC, New Series (Sep 1911) 545–61.

MOORE, GEORGE, 'The Irish Literary Theatre', *Samhain* (Dublin) (Oct 1901) 11–13.

MORROW, GERALD, 'The Belfast Theatre', *The Bell* (Dublin), III, No. 5 (1942) 361–2.
'The Belfast Theatre', *The Bell* (Dublin), IV, No. 1 (1942) 55–6.
'The Belfast Theatre', *The Bell* (Dublin), IV, No. 4 (1942) 301–2.
'The Theatre: Belfast', *The Bell* (Dublin), V, No. 3 (1942) 238–41.

MORROW, GERRY, 'An Ulster Arts Theatre', *Lagan*, No. 2 [n.d. *circa* 1945] 100–1.

MOSELEY, VIRGINIA, 'Week A in Dublin', *Modern Drama* (Lawrence, Kansas), IV, No. 2 (Sep 1961) 164–71.

MOSES, MONTROSE J., 'W. B. Yeats and the Irish Players', *The Metropolitan Magazine* (N.Y.), XXXV, No. 3 (Jan 1912) 23–5, 61–2.
'Dramatists without a Country', *The Book-News Monthly* (Philadelphia) (Feb 1912) 408–9.

'Mr Roosevelt As a Critic', *The Literary Digest* (N.Y.), XLIV, No. 8 (24 Feb 1912) 375–6.

MURPHY, DANIEL J., 'Yeats and Lady Gregory: A Unique Collaboration', *Modern Drama* (Lawrence, Kansas), VII, No. 3 (Dec 1964) 322–8.

NATHAN, GEORGE JEAN, 'Lament for Irish Playwrights', *The American Mercury* (N.Y.), LII, No. 208 (Apr 1941) 483–9.

Neil, J. Crawford, 'Notes on the Celtic Renaissance', *Milwaukee News* (Feb 1911 to 21 Mar 1912).

'New Abbey Theatre by End of 1960', *The Irish Times* (Dublin) (22 Oct 1958) pp. 1, 7.

'New Irish Plays Produced', *The Gael* (N.Y.) (May 1902).

'A New Thing in the Theater: Some Impressions of the Much-Discussed "Irish Players"', *Harper's Weekly* (N.Y.), IV (9 Dec 1911) 19.

Norwood, Gilbert, 'English Drama between Two Wars', *Dalhousie Review*, XXII (Jan 1943) 405–20.

Observer, 'Press Cuttings', *Irish Book Lover* (Dublin), XV, No. 1 (Jan 1925) 16.

O'Carroll, Michael, 'Drama in the New Age', *Iris Hibernia* (Fribourg, Switzerland), IV, No. 3 (1960) 15–19.

O'Connor, Frank, 'The Future of Irish Literature', *Horizon* (London), V, No. 25 (Jan 1942) 55–63.
'All the Olympians', *The Saturday Review* (N.Y.), XLIX, No. 50 (10 Dec 1966) 30–2, 99. [On Synge, Yeats and Lady Gregory.] Reprinted in *The Backward Look: A Survey of Irish Literature* (London: Macmillan, 1967) 183–93.

O'Connor, Ulick, 'Dublin's Dilemma', *Theatre Arts* (N.Y.), XL, No. 7 (July 1956) 64–5, 96.

O'Donnell, Donat, 'The Abbey: Phoenix Infrequent', *The Commonweal* (N.Y.), LVII (30 Jan 1953) 423–4.

O'Faolain, Sean, 'The Abbey Festival', *The New Statesman and Nation* (London), XVI (20 Aug 1938) 281–2.
'The Dilemma of Irish Letters', *Month* (London), II, New Series, No. 6 (Dec 1949) 366–79.
'Ireland After Yeats', *The Bell* (Dublin), XVIII, No. 11 (Summer 1953) 37–48. Reprinted from *Books Abroad* (Norman, Okl.), XXVI, No. 4 (Autumn 1952) 325–33.

O FARACHAIN, ROIBEARD, 'The Second Spring: A Manifesto for the New Abbey Theatre', in the souvenir programme to mark the occasion of the opening of the new Abbey Theatre.

O'HOGARTY, P. S., 'The Abbey Theatre', *The Irish Times* (Dublin) (6 Sep 1944) p. 3. [Letter to the Editor.]

O'MALLEY, MARY, 'Theatre in Belfast', *Iris Hibernia* (Fribourg, Switzerland), IV, No. 3 (1960) 55–7.
'Irish Theatre Letter', *Massachusetts Review*, VI (1964–5) 181–6.

O'NEILL, GEORGE, 'The Inauguration of the Irish Literary Theatre', *The New Ireland Review* (Dublin), XI (June 1899) 246–52.
'Recent Irish Drama and Its Critics', *The New Ireland Review* (Dublin), XXV (Mar 1906) 29–36.
'Some Aspects of Our Anglo-Irish Poets: The Irish Literary Theatre; Foreign Inspiration of Alleged Irish Plays', *The Irish Catholic* (Dublin), XXIV, No. 51 (23 Dec 1911) 5. [Lecture delivered before the National Literary Society, Dublin.]
'Abbey Theatre Libels', *American Catholic Quarterly* (Philadelphia), XXXVII, No. 146 (Apr 1912) 322–32. Reprinted in *The Irish Catholic* (Dublin), XXV, No. 33 (31 Aug 1912), 6; and XXV, No. 34 (7 Sep 1912) 6.

O'RYAN, AGNES, 'The Drama of the Abbey Theatre', *The Irish Educational Review* (Dublin), VI, No. 3 (Dec 1912) 154–63.

PAGE, SEAN, 'The Abbey Theatre', *The Dublin Magazine*, V, Nos. 3–4 (Autumn–Winter 1966) 6–14.

PETTET, E. B., 'Report on the Irish Theatre', *Educational Theatre Journal*, VIII (May 1956) 109–14.

'The Players', *Everybody's Magazine* (N.Y.), XXVI (Feb 1912) 231–40.

PERIODICALS

POWELL, YORK, 'A Fragment of Irish Literary History: Irish Influence on English Literature', *The Freeman's Journal* (Dublin), cxxxv (8 Apr 1902) 6. [Lecture delivered before the National Literary Society, Dublin.]

QUINN, JOHN, 'Lady Gregory and the Abbey Theatre', *The Outlook* (N.Y.), IC (16 Dec 1911) 916–19.

RHODES, RAYMOND CROMPTON, 'The Irish National Theatre', *T. P.'s Weekly* (London), xxI, No. 545 (18 Apr 1913) 504. [Letter to the Editor.]

ROBERTS, PETER, 'Dublin 2', *Plays and Players* (London), xvIII, No. 8 (May 1971) 53–5.

ROBINSON, LENNOX, 'The Birth of a Nation's Theatre', *The Emerson Quarterly* (Boston), xIII, No. 2 (Jan 1933) 3–4, 16–18, 20.

ROOSEVELT, THEODORE, 'In the Eyes of Our Friends: The Irish Theatre', *The Outlook* (N.Y.) (16 Dec 1911) 915 ff.

'Roosevelt As a Critic', *The Literary Digest* (N.Y.), xLIV (24 Feb 1912) 375–6.

ROSENFIELD, RAY, 'Theatre in Belfast: Achievement of a Decade', *Threshold*, II, No. 1 (1958) 66–77.

ROY, JAMES A., 'J. M. Synge and the Irish Literary Movement', *Anglia* (Halle), xxxvII, New Series xxv (1913) 129–45.

RUTTLEDGE, PAUL, 'Stage Management in the Irish National Theatre', *Dana* (Dublin), No. 5 (Sep 1904) 150–2.

RYAN, STEPHEN, 'Theatre in Dublin', *America* (N.Y.), xCII (30 Oct 1954) 128–9.

'Crisis in Irish Letters; Literary Life in Dublin', *The Commonweal* (N.Y.), LxxI, No. 12 (18 Dec 1959) 347–9.

'Ireland and Its Writers', *The Catholic World* (N.Y.), CxcII (1960) 149–55.

SAMPSON, MARTIN W., 'The Irish Literary Theatre', *The Nation* (N.Y.), LxxIII (21 Nov 1901) 395–6.

45

SCUDDER, VIDA D., 'The Irish Literary Drama', *Poet Lore* (Philadelphia), XVI (1905) 40–53.

SEARS, WILLIAM P., Jr., 'New Dublin Players' Group Challenges Abbey Theatre', *The Literary Digest* (N.Y., CXVII, No. 23 (9 June 1934) 26.

SHERIDAN, JOHN D., 'Irish Writing Today', *Studies: An Irish Quarterly Review* (Dublin), XLIV (Spring 1955) 81–5.

SIGERSON, GEORGE, 'The Irish Peasantry and the Stage', *United Irishman* (Dublin) (17 Feb 1906) 2–3.

SILKE, ELIZABETH, 'Drama in Belfast', *The Bell* (Dublin), XV, No. 4 (1948) 65–7.

SKEFFINGTON, F. SHEEHY, 'The Irish National Theatre', *T. P.'s Weekly* (London), XXI, No. 547 (2 May 1913) 566. [Letter to the Editor.]

SKELTON, ROBIN, 'Twentieth-Century Irish Literature and the Private Press Tradition: Dun Emer, Cuala, and Dolmen Presses, 1902–1963', *Massachusetts Review*, V (1964) 368–77.

SMITH, HUGH, 'Twilight of the Abbey?' *The New York Times* (31 Mar 1935), Section XI, p. 2.

SMITH, PAUL, 'Dublin's Lusty Theater', *Holiday* (Philadelphia), XXXIII (April 1963) 119 f.

'Stage Workshop', *The Times Literary Supplement* (London) (28 Aug 1959) p. 495. [Editorial.]

'A State Theatre', *The Irish Press* (Dublin) (22 May 1947) p. 4. [Editorial.]

STEWART, ANDREW J., 'The Acting of the Abbey Theatre', *Theatre Arts Monthly* (N.Y.), XVII, No. 3 (Mar 1933) 243–5.

'The Stormy Debut of the Irish Players', *Current Literature* (N.Y.), LI (Dec 1911) 675–6.

'The Story of the Irish Players', *Sunday Record-Herald* (Chicago) (4 Feb 1912) Part 7, p. 1.

TENNYSON, CHARLES, 'Irish Plays and Playwrights', *Quarterly Review* (London), CCXV, No. 428 (July 1911) 219–43.

'The Rise of the Irish Theatre', *The Contemporary Review* (London), C (Aug 1911) 240–7.

'Theatre in Dublin', *The Dublin Magazine*, V, Nos. 3–4 (Autumn–Winter 1966) 3–5. [Editorial.]

TOBIN, MICHAEL, 'The Ponderings of a Playgoer', *Iris Hibernia* (Fribourg, Switzerland), IV, No. 3 (1960) 27–39.

TONSON, JACOB, 'Books and Persons', *The New Age* (London), IX, No. 16 (17 Aug 1911) 374–5.

TOWNSHEND, GEORGE, 'The Irish Drama', *Drama Magazine* (Chicago) (Autumn 1911) 93–104.

'Ulster Books and Authors 1900–1953', *Rann*, No. 20 (1953) 55–73.

'Vital Drama', *The Times Literary Supplement* (London) (13 Apr 1940) p. 183. [Editorial.]

W., J., 'The Ulster Literary Theatre', *Ulad: A Literary and Critical Magzaine* (Belfast), I, No. 2 (Feb 1905) 4–8.

'The Theatre and the People', *Ulad: A Literary and Critical Magazine* (Belfast), I, No. 3 (May 1905) 13–14.

WALBROOK, H. M., 'The Irish Dramatists and Their Countrymen', *The Fortnightly Review* (London), C (Nov 1913) 957–61. Reprinted in *The Living Age* (Boston), CCLXXIX (27 Dec 1913) 789–93.

WALSH, LOUIS J., 'A Catholic Theatre for Dublin', *Irish Rosary* (Dublin), XXXIX (Oct 1935) 749–54.

WATKINS, ANN, 'The Irish Players in America: Their Purpose and Their Art', *Craftsman* (N.Y.), XXI (Jan 1912) 352–63.

WEBBER, JOHN E., 'The Irish Players', *The Canadian Magazine* (Toronto), XXXVIII (Mar 1912) 471–81.

WEYGANDT, CORNELIUS, 'The Art of the Irish Players and a Comment on Their Plays', *The Book-News Monthly* (Philadelphia) (Feb 1912) 379–81.

'The Irish Literary Revival', *Sewanee Review*, XII, No. 4 (Oct 1904) 420–31.

'What's Wrong with the Abbey?' *Plays and Players* (London), X, No. 5 (Feb 1963) 22–4.

WHEELER, ETHEL ROLT, 'Ideals in Irish Poetry and Drama', *Irish Book Lover* (Dublin and London), II, No. 5 (Dec 1910) 79. [Synopsis of lecture delivered on 5 Nov 1910 before the Irish Literary Society, Dublin.]

'The World and the Theatre', *Theatre Arts Monthly* (N.Y.), XIX, No. 12 (Dec 1935) 886.

YEATS, W. B., 'The Celtic Element in Literature', *Cosmopolis* (London), X (June 1898), 675–86. Reprinted in *Essays* (London: Macmillan, 1924) pp. 213–31; and in *Essays and Introductions* (London: Macmillan, 1961) pp. 173–89.

'The Theatre', *The Dome* (London), III (Apr 1899) 48–52.

'The Irish Literary Theatre', *Literature* (London), (6 May 1899) 474.

'The Irish Literary Theatre, 1900', *The Dome* (London), V (Jan 1900) 234–6. Reprinted in *Beltaine* (Dublin), (Feb 1900) 22–4.

'The Irish Drama', *Twentieth Century Magazine* (Boston), V (1911) 12–15.

'A People's Theatre: A Letter to Lady Gregory', *The Dial* (N.Y.), LXVIII, No. 4 (Apr 1920) 458–68.

'A Defence of the Abbey Theatre', *The Dublin Magazine*, I, No. 2 (Apr–June 1926) 8–12. [A speech delivered at a meeting of the Dublin Literary Society, on 23 Feb 1926.]

4. Unpublished Material

Abbey Theatre, Dublin, 'Programmes, 1902–1913', National Library of Ireland, Dublin.

ABOOD, EDWARD F., 'The Reception of the Abbey Theatre in America, 1911–14, PhD Dissertation, University of Chicago, 1963.

ALLT, G. D. P., 'The Anglo-Irish Literary Movement in Relation to Its Antecedents', PhD Dissertation, St Catherine's College, Cambridge University, 1952.

BERNARDBEHAN, BROTHER MERRILL, 'Anglo-Irish Literature', MA Thesis, University of Montreal, 1939.

BERROW, J. H., 'A Study of the Background Treatment and Presentation of Irish Character in British Plays from the Late 19th Century to the Present Day', MA Thesis, University of Wales, Swansea, 1966.

BUTLER, HENRY J., 'The Abbey Theatre and the Principal Writers Connected Therewith', (Aug 1925). MS 2263: The National Library of Ireland, Dublin.

BYARS, JOHN ARTHUR, 'The Heroic Type in the Irish Legendary Dramas of W. B. Yeats, Lady Gregory, and J. M. Synge, 1903–1910', PhD Dissertation, University of North Carolina, 1963.

COLE, A. S., 'Stagecraft in the Modern Dublin Theatre', PhD Dissertation, Trinity College, Dublin, 1953.

COLEMAN, SR ANNE G., 'Social and Political Satire in Irish Drama', PhD Dissertation, Fordham University, 1954.

COOPER, MABEL, 'The Irish Theatre: Its History and Its Dramatists', MA Thesis, University of Manitoba, 1931.

COTTER, EILEEN M., 'The Deirdre Theme in Anglo-Irish Literature', PhD Dissertation, University of California at Los Angeles, 1967.

HENDERSON, WILLIAM A., 'The Irish National Theatre Movement', told in press cuttings. Collected by W. A. Henderson. A Collection in the National Library of Ireland, Dublin, 1899 et seq.

HOLLOWAY, JOSEPH, 'Impressions of a Dublin Playgoer', MSS at the National Library of Ireland, Dublin: MS 1877, Apr–June 1923; MS 1881, Sep–Dec 1923; MS 1884, Jan–Mar 1924; MS 1885, Apr–June 1924; MS 1886, Apr–June 1924; MS 1888, July–Sep 1924; MS 1889, Oct–Dec 1924; MS 1892, Jan–Mar 1925; MS 1898, Oct–Dec 1925; MS 1899, Jan–Mar 1926; MS 1900, Jan–Mar 1926.

HOLZAPFEL, R. P., 'A Survey of Irish Literary Periodicals from 1900 to the Present Day', MLitt Thesis, Trinity College, Dublin, 1963.

KELSON, JOHN HOFSTAD, 'Nationalism in the Theater: The Ole Bull Theater in Norway and the Abbey Theater in Ireland: A Comparative Study', PhD Dissertation, University of Kansas, 1964.

'Little Theatre, Belfast', Bound Collection of programmes 1933–1935. Queen's University Library, Belfast.

LYMAN, KENNETH C., 'Critical Reaction to Irish Drama on the New York Stage, 1900–1958', PhD Dissertation, University of Wisconsin, 1960.

MCGUIRE, JAMES BRADY, 'Realism in Irish Drama', PhD Dissertation, Trinity College, Dublin, 1954.

UNPUBLISHED MATERIAL

McHenry, Margaret, 'The Ulster Theatre in Ireland', PhD Dissertation, University of Pennsylvania, 1931.

O'Neill, Michael J., 'The Diaries of a Dublin Playgoer as a Mirror of the Irish Literary Revival', PhD Dissertation, National University, Dublin, 1952.

Peteler, Patricia M., 'The Social and Symbolic Drama of the English-Language Theatre, 1929–1949', PhD Dissertation, University of Utah, 1961.

Randall, Ethel Claire, 'The Celtic Movement; The Awakening of the Fires', MA Thesis, University of Chicago, 1906.

Saddlemyer, E. A., 'A Study of the Dramatic Theory Developed by the Founders of the Irish Literary Theatre and the Attempt to Apply This Theory in the Abbey Theatre, with Particular Reference to the Achievement of the Major Figures during the First Two Decades of the Movement', PhD Dissertation, Bedford College, University of London, 1961.

Smyth, Dorothy Pearl, 'The Playwrights of the Irish Literary Renaissance', MA Thesis, Acadia University, 1936.

Suss, Irving David, 'The Decline and Fall of Irish Drama', PhD Dissertation, Columbia University, 1951.

Thompson, William I., 'Easter 1916: A Study in Literature and Revolution', PhD Dissertation, Cornell University, 1966.

Wickstrom, Gordon M., 'The Deirdre Plays of AE, Yeats, and Synge: Patterns of Irish Exile', PhD Dissertation, Stanford University, 1969.

Worth, Katharine J., 'Symbolism in Modern English Drama', PhD Dissertation, University of London, 1953.